Bibliographical Series
of Supplements to 'British Book News'
on Writers and Their Work

★

GENERAL EDITOR
Geoffrey Bullough

SHELLEY

from a portrait of 1819 by AMELIA CURRAN *in
the National Portrait Gallery*

SHELLEY

by

STEPHEN SPENDER

PUBLISHED FOR
THE BRITISH COUNCIL
AND THE NATIONAL BOOK LEAGUE
BY LONGMANS, GREEN & CO.

LONGMANS, GREEN & CO. LTD.
48 Grosvenor Street, London W.1

*Associated companies, branches and
representatives throughout the world*

*First published 1952
Reprinted with additions to bibliography 1960, 1964*
© Stephen Spender, 1960

*Printed in Great Britain by
F. Mildner & Sons, London, E.C.1*

SHELLEY

I

THE man in whom his countrymen least recognize their own image, may nevertheless have many qualities which are characteristic of them. Thus the boy who was known to his Eton contemporaries as 'mad Shelley' was typical in many ways of a certain type of poetical English aristocrat. His youthful desire to identify himself with a revolutionary cause, his discovery within himself of original powers of judgement whereby he examined, as though for the first time, every existing social institution, his fads and eccentricities, and his perpetual adolescence, are recurrent qualities among the English upper classes. It is no mere chance that in every poetic generation critics discover some poet who qualifies to be 'another Shelley'. 'An ineffectual angel', Matthew Arnold called him; and this verdict seems made by a judge who feels proud of having grown to attain efficacity.

Moreover, those opinions which made Shelley such a controversial figure in his lifetime are still argued for and against to-day. One contemporary critic, T. S. Eliot, repudiated Shelley for the famous lines, attacking marriage, and defending free love, in 'Epipsychidion', in the passage which begins:

> I never was attached to that great sect,
> Whose doctrine is that each one should select
> Out of the world a mistress or a friend . . .

But if Eliot condemned these views by conservative standards, another great modern, Bernard Shaw, tells us that he became a socialist as a result of reading Shelley. Shelley is one of the very few English poets to have been taken to heart by many workers in the Labour Movement. The ideas which agitated him so violently are, for the most part, still living issues, and that is perhaps why we are almost as far from making a final evaluation of his work to-day as critics were a hundred years ago. Owing to his early death, the anxiety of his widow to preserve every fragment of his poetry, and his carelessness as an artist, his Collected Works are like a garden in which the weeds choke a good many of the flowers. His faults militate against his virtues, and his life work is a muddied stream. And his personal life— his youthful rebelliousness against his father, his atheism which caused him to be expelled from Oxford, his first marriage followed by the suicide of his young wife, his tangled relationships with people as different as his Oxford friend Hogg and the father-in-law of his second marriage, Godwin—make his character as controversial as his poetry.

The name Shelley, shining a bright but blurred light in our minds, means at least three strains so intertwined that it is difficult to separate them: his revolutionary theories; his personal life; and his poems.

Vivid reminiscences of Shelley were written by his friends Hogg, Peacock, and Trelawny. It is these por-trayals which have created the legend of a frenetic, excitable youth given to ecstatic enthusiasms and subject to hallucina-tions. Wild as Shelley doubtless was, one must take into account that each of these studies was coloured by senti-ments aroused in the writer by Shelley. Hogg's *Life of Shelley* is the work of a man who feels that at a certain moment he betrayed an idyllic friendship; but that in so doing he took the first step towards growing up into the rather successful, practical lover of the world, who later looks back with a certain irony on the 'divine poet'. Peacock, before writing his recollections of Shelley, in which gentle mockery spreads rainbow lights of affection, had already created two satiric portraits of him in novels: as Mr. Foster in *Headlong Hall*, and Skythrop, the poet who inhabits a lonely tower, in *Nightmare Abbey*. So when he came to write of the real Shelley, a fictitious angle on him was already established in his mind. Edward John Trelawny in his very vivid accounts of the Romantics, adds a dimension of romantic fiction to their romantic poetry.

All this is not to say that these portraits by Shelley's friends are untrue. But with their truth goes the kind of partiality and passion which we find in the recollections by his friends of D. H. Lawrence—a writer who seems to have disturbed those who knew him as much in our day as Shelley did in his. The picture of Shelley in the minds of most readers is surely of the boy of eighteen rather than of the man of twenty-nine, who remarked shortly before he died: 'If I die to-morrow, I have lived to be older than my father.' It is the writer of the Notes to 'Queen Mab' who evokes the idea of Shelley in more minds than the poet of 'Prometheus Unbound' or 'The Triumph of Life'. It is true that Shelley, unlike Wordsworth, Coleridge, and Southey, never went back on his revolutionary principles. Yet there is this important difference between the younger and the older Shelley. The first believed that evil is an external burden imposed on men by human institutions, which can be removed by an external change. The later Shelley had looked far deeper into the heart of man and saw the corruption of power which turns to evil the means intended for good. In 'The Triumph of Life' he writes:

And much I grieved to think how power and will
In opposition rule our mortal day,

And why God made irreconcilable
Good and the means of good; and for despair
I half disdained mine eyes' desire to fill

With the spent vision of the times that were
And scarce have ceased to be.—'Dost thou behold',
Said my guide, 'those spoilers spoiled, Voltaire. . . .'

And there is a famous passage on Rousseau, to the same purpose.

His early view that society was divided into tyrants and priests on the one hand, and the enslaved strugglers towards freedom on the other, deepened into a tragic view of the war between good and evil in the human heart. In his personal life, the young Shelley was a rebel; but the Shelley who died at the age of thirty grew into English literature with some of the qualities of a hero of tragedy.

II

Percy Bysshe Shelley was born on 4 August 1792, at Field Place, near Horsham, in Sussex. He was the son of Sir Timothy and Lady Elizabeth Shelley, and heir to considerable wealth and property. He had adoring younger sisters whom, in his childhood, he entertained by frightening them, and himself, with ghost stories. As a boy at Eton he was derided and known as 'mad Shelley'. Already at school and perhaps earlier, he regarded himself as a victim of persecution; and despite his almost feminine sensibility, he vowed to protect the victims and the weak. A famous passage in the early poem 'Laon and Cythna', relates how one day when he had escaped from the schoolroom where voices

> Were but an echo from a world of woes—
> The harsh and grating strife of tyrants and of foes,

he promised himself:

> I will be wise,
> And just, and free, and mild, if in me lies
> Such power, for I grow weary to behold
> The selfish and the strong still tyrannize
> Without reproach or check.

Above all, Shelley felt persecuted by his father, the baronet, who had the mentality of a hard-headed, practical-minded country squire. Sir Timothy's advice to his younger son, John Shelley, was: 'Never read a book, and you'll grow to be a rich man.' In extenuation, it may be noted that when he said this he was perhaps thinking of Percy Bysshe, whose life demonstrated the exact converse. The father had no sympathy with his elder son's flights of fancy, and still less with his heterodox opinions. In 1840— by when Shelley had the two qualifications which usually reconcile men of genius with their families, of being famous and dead—Sir Timothy put difficulties in the way of the publication of his son's *Collected Poems*, and was obdurately opposed to his biography being written.

So, feeling persecuted by him, Percy Bysshe regarded himself as liberating first his sisters, and later the world, from the 'forces of unreason' represented by his father. The idea of liberating someone aroused passionate feelings in him. It is significant that in both his marriages the idea of freeing a woman from tyrannical circumstances was a strong motive for matrimony.

Shelley went up to Oxford, at University College, in 1810. On his very first evening in college, he struck up a friendship with a fellow undergraduate, Thomas Jefferson Hogg. On Shelley's side this relationship was perhaps the first of a series of friendships in which he sought for someone who would understand him in a way which was almost absolute; someone with whom he could identify himself completely. Hogg, on his side, was the first in a series of rather earth-bound men-friends who found himself uplifted by something ecstatic and angelic in Shelley; something from which he was to react later, rather violently. The subsequent history of this relationship shows that it was rather abnormal on both sides. Shelley sought to involve Hogg in his own relationships with women, and Hogg was a not unwilling accessory to this wish: for, as Winifred Scott, Hogg's recent biographer, puts it, he was for ever in search of a 'she-Shelley'.

The Oxford career of Shelley and Hogg ended in a

fiasco which—because it enters into the biography of a great poet—has become literary history. On a day of March 1811, the windows of Messrs. Munday and Slatter, Oxford booksellers, displayed a pamphlet entitled *The Necessity of Atheism*. They had not been on sale many minutes before the Reverend Mr. John Walker, Fellow of New College, entered the shop, consulted with the proprietors, and supervised the burning of all the copies of the offensive publication in the back kitchen.

The two friends were dealt with almost as decisively as their pamphlet. They were expelled from Oxford. This episode probably crystallized the pattern of the short ten years odd of life remaining to Shelley. If he had stayed at Oxford he would, before going out into the world, have developed beyond the stage where youthful opinions led him into extravagant and sometimes catastrophic behaviour, which, in turn, caused others to persecute him. As it was, his emotions, his impulses, his opinions, his actions, and the reactions of other people to him, were like furies, driving him from place to place.

In the summer of this eventful year, Shelley met and married Harriet Westbrook, the daughter of a London publican. His exposition to Hogg of his reasons for entering into this marriage is highly characteristic of him: 'She had become violently attached to *me*, and I feared that I should not return the attachment. . . . It was impossible to avoid being much affected, I promised to unite my fate with hers. I staid in London some days, during which she recovered her spirits.' Shelley considered Harriet to have been persecuted at school, which he referred to as her 'prison-house'.

The marriage took place at Edinburgh where Shelley, Harriet, and Hogg for a time shared rooms together. After this, they all three went to York, whence Shelley proceeded alone south, in an attempt to patch up things with his father, leaving his young wife and Hogg alone together. During his absence Hogg attempted to seduce Harriet, a fact which Shelley discovered on his return. There was, of course, nothing in Shelley's views on free love to make this wrong, there were only considerations of whether or not Hogg was sacrificing his higher to his lower nature. The two friends moralized over this in a correspondence lasting for months.

Like the expulsion from Oxford, this abrupt episode, while testing the weaknesses of Shelley's philosophy, was also revealing of his psychology. His friendship with Hogg now entered a new and perhaps guilt-haunted phase, as though they had shut themselves out from the paradise of their earlier relationship. Subsequent events indicate that when Shelley left Hogg and Harriet alone together, a side of his nature colluded with Hogg's attempt; it was not Shelley nor Hogg but Harriet whose virtue was demonstrated.

Had not Shelley shared all the experiences of this marriage with his friend? Did he not want Harriet to love Jefferson Hogg and Jefferson to love her? And at what point does such a passion of identification stop? Before the marriage, Shelley had tried to arrange a union between his sister Elizabeth and Jefferson Hogg; and later on, at the time of his elopement with Mary Godwin, who was to become his second wife, he not only suddenly renewed his friendship with Hogg, but advocated a relationship of physical intimacy between her and his friend. Newman Ivey White in his *Life of Shelley* sums the situation up thus: 'It was obviously Shelley's pleasure in beholding her union with Hogg that in Mary's eyes constituted the chief attraction, for both herself and Hogg, in this anticipated union!'

Yet the qualities which caused his detractors to accuse Shelley of immorality and viciousness were surely the excesses of a spiritual rather than a physical nature. What Shelley wanted of a relationship was a situation where another and himself were fused within the white flame of an intense spiritual excitement. The authority which made him a law unto himself and justified him to himself was the ecstacy of his own nature. Perhaps this kind of enthusiasm is as much or even more harmful than the sensuality of a plainer character like Jefferson Hogg. But all the same it is different, and it produced his best poetry. The real dilemma of the moral critic when confronted by a poet like Shelley is that the qualities in his life which make him reprehensible are exactly those which gave him the experience of his poetry. There are indeed moments when his poetry seems a pure jet streaming out of his life:

> Though the sound overpowers,
> Sing again, with your dear voice revealing
> A tone
> Of some world far from ours,
> Where music and moonlight and feeling
> Are one.

The inner meaning of Hogg's extraordinary *Life of Shelley* is the discovery of the legalistically minded biographer that in order that the poet might create in his poetry he must be immensely destructive in his life. And the destructiveness which made so many of his contemporaries condemn Shelley, was in Shelley's own activity pure creativeness.

In both his marriages he entered into relationships of destruction—destructive to him, and destructive to Harriet and perhaps also to Mary. In freer relationships, which produced indeed his most beautiful love poetry—such as 'Epipsychidion', and the beautiful poems to Mary, before he was married to her, and to Jane Williams—his spirit bursts into flame with another before he has reached the stage of destructiveness. It should be noted, however, that Shelley although he could not harmonize what was to him the realest moment of experience with another person, into the long, patient, constructive edifice of a satisfactory marriage, was not so blind to his own nature as to be incapable of a human relationship. His best friends—Hogg, Peacock, Byron, and Sidney Smith—all had a strongly satiric vein and viewed him ironically. On the level of almost cynical companionship, Shelley was a most successful friend. Again, to people like Jane and Edward Williams, who, whilst accepting him, viewed him with a certain detachment, he seemed a man without reproach. And when, as in the case of Godwin, charity and tolerance were required of him, he showed the considerateness of an exemplary Christian. But at his most intense he was dangerous, because when the muse became identified with a human being, he sacrificed the person to the muse.

The three years of Shelley's marriage to Harriet might well be called his 'English period'. At all events it was a time when he confined his wanderings to the British Isles, although as Harriet observed: 'Whenever we fix upon one particular place of residence something comes to take us to another.' The 'something' was usually debts. But on one occasion it was a conviction that a Welsh farmer was bent on assassinating him. Sometimes it was some Cause, such as that of persuading the people of Dublin of the justice of their rights, which led him abroad.

Shelley was already occupied in distributing the wealth which he was heir to by raising money on his prospects, at ruinous rates of interest. He acted on the principle, derived from reading Godwin's *Political Justice*, that it was the duty of an heir to distribute his wealth amongst those who would make the best use of it. Shelley's benevolence ham-strung his life. If his charity was in some ways a rich man's extravagance, he was nevertheless an utterly generous, and, in many ways, a most selfless man. A study of Shelley's gifts as they are listed in Peck's or Ivey White's biography, throws much light on the economic condition of writers who were his contemporaries. Trelawny, in what is hardly excessive indignation, remarks that there was scarcely anyone who knew Shelley who did not try to get money out of him. But in addition to his generosity to men like Leigh Hunt, Peacock, and Godwin, wherever he lived he concerned himself with helping the poor.

'Mad Shelley' was perhaps scarcely less febrile, eccentric,

and whimsical than his contemporaries, who saw him inquire earnestly of a baby as to its prenatal experiences, or
heard the shrillness of his voice when he was excited, or
who were delayed on walks by his passion for sailing paper
boats upon a pond, thought him to be. But perhaps he
had more potentialities than they saw. In a thoughtful
essay on his Oxford career, Edmund Blunden makes the
telling point that had Shelley lived, he would probably have
returned to the Alma Mater. Reading of his charitable
life in Devonshire and Buckinghamshire reveals a side of
him which might have gone well with a country parson.
In his dealings with Godwin and other indebted friends, he
sometimes seems the wisest man in a company of hysterics.
And here is Leigh Hunt's account of his daily life at Marlow
in 1816: 'He was up early, breakfasted sparingly; wrote
. . . all the morning; went out in his boat or into the woods
with some Greek author or the Bible in his hands; came
home to a dinner of vegetables (for he took neither meat
nor wine); visited (if necessary) "the sick and the father-
less", whom others gave Bibles to and no help; wrote or
studied again, or read to his wife and friends the whole
evening; took a crust of bread or a glass of whey for his
supper; and went early to bed.'

III

William Godwin's *Political Justice* profoundly influenced
Shelley not only in earlier works like 'Queen Mab' and 'The
Revolt of Islam', but also in his conduct. His ideas of free
love, his impatience with the unreasonableness of political
and religious institutions which held men in bondage, his
belief in the efficacy of reason in promoting action leading
to a redistribution of worldly goods and offices, his hatred of
priests, tyrants, and rich oppressors, all more or less corre-
sponded with the views of Godwin, from whom he largely
derived them. In 1811 he took an important step. He
wrote to Godwin expressing his debt to *Political Justice*,

and explaining his own situation as a young man with considerable worldly prospects who wished to use his advantages in order to benefit society.

The subsequent relationship between Godwin and Shelley was a tragi-comic nemesis which overtook them both. It resembled the tangled metaphor of the eagle and the serpent (Shelley once addressed a poem to an eagle who is supposedly Godwin and he often referred to himself as the snake), which Shelley expands at such length in 'The Revolt of Islam':

> A course precipitous, of dizzy speed,
>   Suspending thought and breath; a monstrous sight!
> For in the air do I behold indeed
>   An Eagle and a Serpent wreathed in fight:—
>   And now relaxing its impetuous flight,
> Before the aëreal rock on which I stood,
>   The Eagle, hovering, wheeled to left and right,
> And hung with lingering wings over the flood,
> And startled with its yells the wide air's solitude.

The metaphor—extended for seven stanzas—has been excellently discussed in Sir Herbert Read's *In Defence of Shelley*. It is one of the most problematic passages in Shelley; and it also reads like an exact description of the relationship between the mutually destructive poet and philosopher. They met in the empyrean of Utopian idealism, and were equally matched with exalted weapons which, there aloft, each turned against the other. Shelley applied the philosopher's message of free love to the person of his own daughter, whom he bore away from her home; Godwin used the philosophy of the redistribution of wealth for the purpose of entangling the poet in the snares of his own debts.

Mary Shelley had the intellectual power which Harriet seemed to lack. In the early stages of their relationship, each must have been carried away as never before by a sense of understanding and being understood by another person. In their attitude to previous ties they both showed at first an idealistic unrealism which later gave way to idealistic ruthlessness. Shelley suggested that Harriet, Mary, and himself should all three live together, Harriet as his sister, and Mary as his wife. Harriet having proved unworthy of this kind of high-mindedness, Mary and Shelley departed on the first of their European pilgrimages. From Troyes, Shelley wrote to Harriet suggesting that she should join the happy couple; and that she should bring with her the deeds prepared for hers and Shelley's legal separation.

However, Mary did not escape from the Shelleyan idea of a *ménage à trois*. Accompanying them was Claire Clairemont, rejected pursuer of Lord Byron. Claire Clairemont, attached to Shelley by inexorable bonds of misfortune and persecution, was to become the bane of Mary's life. But Mary's father, Godwin, was the old man of the sea around the neck of Shelley.

Harriet committed suicide, and became 'that poor lost creature' in the vocabulary which the Shelleys used to one another. But two anecdotes should serve to check the reader's possible inclination to think of Shelley as beyond the pale of reality. Someone mentioned to Shelley that his life had been described as being like a German romance. 'Very severe', commented Shelley; and then after a moment he added, 'and very just.' On another occasion, Shelley—who was teetotal—remarked to Peacock that he was of a mind to take a great draught of ale every day. Later, at the end of the same afternoon, he explained abruptly: 'I was thinking of Harriet.' The purpose of the draught of ale was to deaden the draught of leaden grief which was his daily lot:

> That time is dead for ever, child!
> Drowned, frozen, dead for ever!
>   We look on the past
>   And stare aghast
> At the spectres wailing, pale and ghast,
> Of hopes which thou and I beguiled
>   To death on life's dark river.

Mary too had her frightful load of death to bear. In one year she lost both her children, Clara and William Shelley, and found that she who had been a mother was no longer one. Her grief at the death of William was of a kind to estrange her from her husband and all her friends. Perhaps too, despite her intellect, her nature was more frivolous than Harriet's had been. After their first ecstasy, a coldness of too many deaths and too heavy loads of guilt and obligation—such as Shelley's interminable involvement with Godwin's debts—froze the marriage.

In his last years Shelley became a solitary in a real sense, and not in the picturesque one of his early poem 'Alastor'. Certainly he was always alone, but one is only a solitary when one accepts the fact of solitude. By law, he had been deprived of the care of his children by Harriet, for whom he, an agnostic and immoralist, was considered unfit as a guardian. Rumours of his irregular life prejudiced nearly every critic against him: 'Shelley—an unmentionable subject' was how his name appeared in the index of one review. But by most he was not even mentioned as unmentionable. A few loyal friends who supported him—Leigh Hunt, for example—yet continued to exploit him to a degree which must have been alienating. His father-in-law robbed and abused him.

His relationships were now of a solitary kind—the companionship he got from Edward Williams, with whom he went sailing, or with that romanticizing ruffian, Trelawny. He was still capable of falling transcendentally in love, as 'Epipsychidion', celebrating his relationship with Emilia Viviani, shows. But the intensely spiritualized passion had now become almost an aesthetic feeling removed from its object; so that when Emilia asked for a sum of money Shelley seemed hardly surprised, and Mary's comment 'So much for Percy's platonics' was not so very far from his own point of view—only he had written his poem out of the situation, a fact whose relevance Mary might not have noticed. Perhaps, indeed, Shelley was always in search of a situation rather than a person: a fellow-persecutee from whom what was required was an intense consciousness of her own situation, which was Shelley's own. Towards the end, Shelley must have realized that his love affairs were occasions which produced an hallucinatory state of mind, which was not a deception so long as it remained what it was—his kind of poetry of living.

In the last months of his life, Shelley had surely attained an equilibrium which was not far from happiness. Perhaps it was even a greater happiness than most people know. Paradoxically, the basis of this happiness was the breakdown of his relationship with Mary. For instead of plunging into another marriage, he accepted the circumstances of his life with kindness, and a certain indifference. His relationship with Jane Williams produced his most touching poetry and yet it came nearest to being a 'shared' relationship, a trio of Jane, Shelley, and her husband. And Newman Ivey White suggests that, in the end, Shelley preferred sailing with Edward to poeticizing his feelings with Jane.

It is difficult not to think that the man who went wandering far into the woods to compose, and whom Trelawny describes having such childlike trust that, when he had been instructed to dive to the bottom of a pond, he lay waiting there until Trelawny plunged in to fetch him up again, was not, in his strange serpentine way, which caused Byron to call him 'the snake', happy. He had learned the comradeship which expects little of others, and perhaps in his attitude to Mary he had acquired something of the irony of Hogg and Peacock. He showed a sense of realism which caused his friends now to go to him for advice as well as money; and he grappled with the complexities of Godwin's debts in a way that might be the envy of a business man. He had put himself at a remove from his old revolutionary fervour, so that although he wished no less to change society, he saw the unchangeable wrong in the hearts of men.

When he entered so enthusiastically into Williams's and

Trelawny's plans for building a yacht, he was perhaps, like D. H. Lawrence at the end of his work, preparing his own 'ship of death'. At any rate, it is difficult to read the story of Shelley's last year without feeling that he already knew, in some way, its culmination.

The story of the capsizing of the *Don Juan* off Lerici in the second week of July 1822 is well known. Shelley and Williams were both drowned. Shelley's body, having been thrown up on the shore, was burned on a huge funeral pyre, with Byron and Trelawny as witnesses. Trelawny describes how he snatched the heart out of the burning body. After considerable difficulty, Mary managed to obtain this, of which she considered herself the rightful owner. She kept it in a small parcel on her desk, while she wrote novel after novel, regurgitating her early experiences through a Victorian era, in which many of Shelley's desired improvements to society took place, in the most materialist environment the world had seen. Hogg subsequently married Jane, the widow of Edward Williams, uniting himself thus with Shelley's last love, after the poet's death.

The world of his contemporaries was not altogether wrong about Shelley. A self-deceiver, if he was forced into an untenable situation he became a cad, as in his treatment of Harriet. Even his warmest admirers discerned a streak of disingenuousness in his truth-loving nature. Yet self-deceivers meet with general condemnation because they are bad men deceiving themselves that they are good. Shelley was the case of a good man, with occasional lapses, who in the intensity of his vision of virtue deceived himself that he was always good. He is abominable when he takes a high moral line with Hogg whom he left in York with every opportunity to seduce Harriet, for attempting to do so; and he is still more abominable when he takes a still higher line over the 'fallen woman' Harriet—fallen like Ophelia, because she was purely devoted to this aristocratic Hamlet. But usually he did live on heights of virtue, which perhaps partly excuses his not knowing where he was when

he had dropped down from them suddenly. Given
conditions in which he was free to act according to his
nature, he struck men as different as Byron, Leigh Hunt, and
Peacock as the best man they had known. A situation in
which he acted badly was one in which he felt his nature
to be curbed. It is significant that amongst his friends it was
the men—Byron, Hunt, Peacock, Trelawny, Williams, and
Medwin—who were most struck by his gentleness, courage,
humour, generosity—and by something more than all
these, an angelic quality. Hogg speaks of Shelley as a
'ladies' man', but he seems to have made more sense when
he was among men.

Shelley knew well that he was two men, a man and a
poet. This is a dangerous knowledge, especially when
applied to men who are not poets but who think they are.
Yet it is certainly true of a poet like Shelley that one of the
characters in his double-personality was a man trying out
the crude material of his poetry crudely in his life; the
other, the poet who purifies, moulds, and transforms this
material in his work. The man Shelley had the shrill,
excitable voice which jarred on the ears of several hearers
(they still complain to posterity about it): the poet has a
voice which wins readers by the thrilling purity of its
music. The political thinker and activist, Shelley lived out
ideas which often seem staring caricatures of themselves in
his example: the poet was engaged in a perpetual struggle
to express these ideas in vivid and impassioned imaginative
language, so that they might pierce beneath the surface
habit of thinking of his readers, to a deeper level where
human existences are bound together in love, and thus
change men by giving them a new and truer view of their
natures, so that they in turn might change society.

IV

Shelley wrote—directly and indirectly—a good deal about
what he considered the function of poetry to be. There is

no better way of examining his own poetry than by considering first of all some of these aims, and then comparing
them with his achievement.

The mine of all his views is contained in the famous essay
'A Defence of Poetry', which contains the challenging and
challenged statement that 'poets are the unacknowledged
legislators of the world'. His argument is that the roots of
human institutions lie in the imaginative life of humanity,
so that the animation of this life by poetry will affect institutions. He is surely not wrong in making this general
claim. The law of the Old Testament is very close to the
poetry of the prophets. The self-visioning of England by
the English which has sent generations of the young to the
ends of the earth, and which has inspired again and again
the defence of their island from opponents, is to an incal-
culable extent owing to Shakespeare, Milton, and Wordsworth. Perhaps it is the incalculableness of the effect of the
poet on legislation which makes Shelley's statement objec-
tionable to some minds. Or perhaps it is the poet's idea
that in this lies the defence of poetry. Herrick's poem
about 'a sweet disorder in the dress' may have affected
sartorial fashion, but one cannot imagine Herrick defending
his poem on these grounds. He was simply occupied in
making an object, a poem, without regard to its effect.
Shelley certainly represents a tendency of poets to have their
eyes not on their poems, but on the effects of their poetry.
On the other hand, Shakespeare in his sonnets makes
extravagant worldly claims for his poetry, and both Milton
and Wordsworth regarded themselves as 'unacknowledged
legislators', if not as something much grander. Too much
has been made of an effective phrase which is neither so
original nor so controversial as some critics seem to imagine.

The core of Shelley's belief about poetry lies in the
following passage from the same essay:

> We have more moral, political, and historical wisdom than we know
> how to reduce into practice; we have more scientific and economic
> knowledge than can be accommodated to the just distribution of the

produce which it multiplies. The poetry in these systems of thought, is
concealed by the accumulation of facts and calculating processes. . . .
We want the creative faculty to imagine that which we know.

'Imagine that which we know.' By this, Shelley
means creating in poetry a language of the imagination
which may include the enormous advances in specialized
knowledge of the modern age. Thus poetry may become a
meeting-place of the forces most affecting a modern society.
Such a poetry would be at the same time modern and
traditional. Poetry would be continuously revolutionized
by the new life of modern men, and at the same time it
would retain that traditionalist position at the centre of
social forces which it has had in the great ages of literature.

So that in Shelley's view poetry should be an instrument
which translates specialized branches of knowledge and
specialized activities of modern life into one symbolic
language where all these separate activities meet within the
life of the imagination. But at the same time, Shelley
remembers that the poet is an individual with particular
tastes decided by his own personality, that is by his individual capacity for love:

Poetry enlarges the circumference of the imagination by replenishing
it with thoughts of ever new delight, which have the power of attracting
and assimilating to their own nature all other thoughts, and which form
new intervals and interstices whose void for ever craves fresh food.
Poetry strengthens that faculty which is the organ of the moral nature
of man, in the same manner as exercise strengthens a limb. A poet
therefore would do ill to embody his own conceptions of right and
wrong, which are usually those of his place and time, in his poetical
creations, which participate in neither.

This, written in 1821, shows how far Shelley had travelled
in the eight years since he wrote the didactic 'Queen Mab'.

Of all his work, the one in which he was most successful
in fulfilling his own poetic ideal is undoubtedly 'Prometheus
Unbound'. For there he creates poetry enclosing in its references the whole range of his considerable knowledge. He

pursued his own vein of fantasy without inhibition, and without forcing himself into didactic channels; and the subject he chose—the liberation of Prometheus (humanity) from his enchainment by Jupiter (tyranny of rulers and beliefs)— is ennobling and beautiful in the highest degree. The famous lines in the Third Act show Shelley's poetry functioning according to his ideal vision of his poetic function:

> None frowned, none trembled, none with eager fear
> Gazed on another's eye of cold command,
> Until the subject of a tyrant's will
> Became, worse fate, the abject of his own,
> Which spurred him, like an outspent horse, to death.
> None wrought his lips in truth-entangling lines
> Which smiled the lie his tongue disdained to speak;
> None, with firm sneer, trod out in his own heart
> The sparks of love and hope till there remained
> Those bitter ashes, a soul self-consumed,
> And the wretch crept a vampire among men,
> Infecting all with his own hideous ill;
> None talked that common, false, cold, hollow talk
> Which makes the heart deny the *yes* it breathes,
> Yet question that unmeant hypocrisy
> With such a self-mistrust as has no name.
> And women, too, frank, beautiful, and kind
> As the free heaven which rains fresh light and dew
> On the wide earth, past; . . . .

This passage—and the whole speech by the Spirit of the Hour, from which it comes—is one of those rare examples—found rarely also in Wordsworth—in which a poet's theories about the function of poetry suddenly fuse with his inspiration. The structure of the thought has an extreme simplicity which is illustrated with rich complexity. It contrasts the negation of a certain kind of life with its opposite, the assertion of another life. The overthrow of Jupiter by Prometheus in the poetic drama is supposed to have freed the positive virtues of living from the freezing social lies which are negative. Here Shelley creates in his poetry the microcosm of a change within society which is supposed to transform the world; and within the same imaginative act he is able to draw vividly upon his impressive knowledge of science, as well as of classical mythology, to illustrate the change. The poetry is like a surgical instrument which can be felt to cut and lay bare the rotten flesh in lines like:

> None wrought his lips in truth-entangling lines
> Which smiled the lie his tongue disdained to speak.

At the same time the surgeon is able imaginatively to cure —to assert, that is to say, the positive which is the opposite of the destructive tissue on which he has performed his operation. The heart breathes its '*yes*'.

Like Wordsworth's, Shelley's theories often had a perverse effect on his poetry. He was burning with enthusiasm to change the world, and he knew the way in which the world should be changed. It was his duty to make men reasonable by stimulating their imaginations. In his early days he confused political enthusiasm with poetic inspiration. Quite apart from this he suffered from an impatience to see his work in print, so that even a work like 'Prometheus Unbound' is vitiated by the lack of patience which could have 'loaded every rift with gold', as Keats wrote to Shelley.

There is often in Shelley's poetry a kind of collapse of his inspiration, with the result that he cannot bring the poem to a satisfactory end: if indeed he can end it at all, for many of his poems are unfinished. The collapse seems sometimes the dissolution of the poet's spirit into sheer invisibility, as in the end of 'Epipsychidion':

> The wingèd words on which my soul would pierce
> Into the height of love's rare Universe,
> Are chains of lead around its flight of fire—
> I pant, I sink, I tremble, I expire!

Or those endings which are too conclusive, like the last lines of 'Prometheus Unbound':

This, like thy glory, Titan, is to be
Good, great and joyous, beautiful and free;
This is alone Life, Joy, Empire, and Victory.

The collapse, paradoxically, is due to the ending of a poem being too final. In the one case, the fainting or expiration of the poet at the end of his poem is more than the reader expects, or than a poem should be allowed to achieve. In the other case, the vision of a world transformed from total misery into total happiness is too complete. In both cases the conclusions lead us away from the poem to a contemplation of a reality which is supposed to have been affected by the poetry—the poet himself, or the world.

All that is demanded of a poet is that he should complete his poem, not that he should finish himself off or add the final touches to Utopia in his poetry. Yet Shelley's poetry is straining beyond itself into a world of events which, though they may be influenced by art, cannot be identified with the single work of art. Putting it quite crudely, if a poet were really to faint writing his poem he would not be able to write that he was fainting while writing it; and if the world were really being transformed into everlasting beauty, he probably would not be writing poetry either. There is a divorce between art and actuality or, at any rate, a marriage in which the relationship between the two is governed by the realization that they deal with different kinds of reality. Shelley was one of those poets who found it very difficult to see the difference between the truth of actuality and the truth of poetry.

On the level of the actuality in which he lived he knew, or thought he knew, all sorts of truths which he wished to introduce into his poems. But for the purposes of his poetry, the deep conviction that man must be freed from bonds of unreason was not enough. It was only a known idea, not an experience derived from living. Shelley's 'known ideas' were continually racing ahead of his experience of living; and yet his mind kept on telling him that his living could only lead to the idealist conclusions which were the results of his philosophic thinking. The Shelleyan collapses occur either when the known ideas seize control of the poetry and deliver a lecture on political philosophy to the poet's limited experience, or when the poet feels completely incapable of living that which he 'knows'. For on the level of his knowledge he is a revolutionary optimist, while on the level of his actual experience he is a disappointed man.

The history of Shelley's development is the gradual taming of his 'known ideas' by his increasing experience. He died before the conflict—which may have killed him—was resolved. Yet out of this conflict was created his greatest poetry in 'Prometheus Unbound' and 'The Triumph of Life'. Moreover, ultimately the conflict was capable of being resolved by a fusion of Shelley's ideas with his experience. His experience of life tended to modify his abstract ideas with concrete reality, whilst the strength of his ideas prevented him from reacting from the revolutionary position of his youth into an opposite position of conservatism, as the Lake poets had done.

V

Shelley was at once an eloquently public-spirited and an intensely personal man. These two aspects of his personality provoke a very marked division in his poetry. As Mary rather primly comments in her 'Note on Alastor': "'Alastor' is written in a very different tone from "Queen Mab". In the latter, Shelley poured out all the cherished speculations of his youth—all the irrepressible emotions of sympathy, censure, and hope, to which the present suffering, and what he considers the proper destiny, of his fellow-creatures, gave birth. "Alastor", on the contrary, contains an individual interest only.'

This division between a poem like 'Queen Mab' and one like 'Alastor' produces further divisions. To simplify the arrangement of material in this brief essay, I shall divide the poems into five categories. Thus:

(1) Didactic poems.
(2) Spiritual autobiographies.
(3) Pure lyrics.
(4) Confessional lyrics.
(5) Satiric poems.

This division is rather arbitrary, and to some extent the divisions overlap. For instance, the satiric poems have a didactic purpose, and a lyric poem like the 'Ode to the West Wind' has a confessional aspect. All the same, 'The Mask of Anarchy' is a very different affair from 'Queen Mab', and a poem like 'The Cloud' has an objective quality lacking in, say, 'The Invitation'.

(1) *Didactic poems.* The earliest and most proselytizing of his poems with a social purpose is Queen Mab. It opens with a haunting passage which has the surpassing beauty which very few poets beside Shelley have achieved at the age of eighteen:

> How wonderful is Death,
> Death and his brother Sleep!

These lines in which Shelley evokes the Faery atmosphere in which he proposes to sublimate a political tract are as unforgettable as 'She walks in beauty like the night', or 'A thing of Beauty is a joy for ever'. They are certainly one of the highest of the peaks of Romantic poetry, though they owe much to Southey's 'Thalaba' which, as late as 1815, Mary described as Shelley's 'favourite poem'.

The young Shelley's aim was to enclose a particular, social, and political contemporary propaganda within a universal vision of history, which in turn was enclosed within a fantastic fairy story. But after two opening sections in which he allows his imagination to wander freely, the reader is pulled up short and the Fairy proceeds to deliver a series of lectures on history, politics, economy, and science. All the same, 'Queen Mab' retains its impression of being struck off at a sitting by a boy inspired with the audacity and confidence of his ideas. It fails to achieve its purpose of melting a political vision within a poetic one. But it remains one of the most daring experiments in the poetry of the past two hundred years.

Shelley's next revolutionary pamphlet, 'The Revolt of Islam', spreads itself over twelve Cantos in Spenserian stanzas. It is a wandering poem, whose purpose is described by Shelley as follows: 'It is a succession of pictures illus-' trating the growth and progress of individual mind aspiring after excellence, and devoted to the love of mankind; its influence in refining and making pure the most daring and uncommon impulses of the imagination, the understanding, and the senses; its impatience at "all the oppressions that lie under the sun"; its tendency to awaken public hope, and to enlighten and improve mankind' . . . and a lot more besides. It opens with a survey of the main events of the French Revolution, and then continues with the story of the hero and heroine, Laon and Cythna. This confused and confusing poem is like an overgrown wilderness, in which are to be found muskets, pikes, helmets, and all the instruments of oppression and revolution, as well as roses and lilies running wild.

The lyrical drama 'Prometheus Unbound' is far and away the most successful of those poems in which Shelley attempts to celebrate the triumph of reason and liberty. In this play, Shelley diverges from the story of the lost drama of Æschylus, in which Prometheus becomes reconciled with his oppressor, Jupiter. Shelley's poem is the story of the triumph of Prometheus over 'the oppressor of mankind'.

As a play, the poem need not be discussed. It is not at all dramatic, perhaps because Shelley did not see so much a drama in the situation of the struggle between gods, as an occasion for the victory of the symbol of the oppressed.

This poem is not even enough a narration to be a pageant. It is a kind of tapestry in which picture after picture is displayed in order to illustrate certain world situations. Where it gains greatly over all Shelley's other attempts to create a work of art out of his social vision, is in the depersonalization of his characters. Shelley had little understanding of individual human beings—or at all events he lacked the creative power to invent a human character in poetry. But he had a real grasp of the forces that move through the lives of people. So long as he is simply using personality as a mask to cover what are really symbols of abstract forces moving through history, he becomes convincing. His grasp of forces extends also to a grasp of scientific principles and inanimate nature, both of which he is able to give that personality which he could never invent in portraits of mere human beings. Shelley could never have written a domestic drama, but he might well have written one in which the sun and moon would have appeared as convincing, and almost human, characters. The true scene of his vision was the whole of human history and the physical universe.

So in 'Prometheus Unbound', the bowed Prometheus, the Earth, Asia, Panthea, and Jupiter, really exist. It is a cosmic lyric, like Schiller's 'Song of Joy' or the Second Part of Goethe's 'Faust'. In certain respects, Shelley developed modern poetry further in this poem than it has gone since. For one aim of modern poetry is surely to make the enormously extended knowledge of the universe gained by science, conscious and significant in our minds. In 'Prometheus Unbound' Shelley links up scientific discovery with the struggle for human liberty.

Of course, it is not fashionable to regard Shelley as a 'modern poet'. 'Modern poetry', as practised by our contemporaries, is concerned above all with writing in new forms and in a contemporary idiom. Shelley probably wrote poetry much as he talked—that is to say, better than he talked—but he did not talk like other men, and only in a

few poems—such as 'The Mask of Anarchy'—did he attempt
to write idiomatically. He was a prolific inventor of forms,
but they are not forms in which anyone is interested
to-day. So he is not regarded as a 'modern poet' by contemporary critics. But the 'modern poets' in their pre-
occupation with form and idiom have given up Shelley's
attempt to create within poetry a subject-matter which
'imagines that which we know'. It is considered 'modern'
to put slang or references to jazz or the London Underground
in a poem, but it is no longer considered modern to attempt
to express in poetry the effect on our vision, say, of Einstein's
theories of the nature of space.

A picture of Prometheus not so much as a man chained
to a mountain rock, but as a mountainous form of aspiring
life, gives 'Prometheus Unbound' a pervading atmosphere of
huge mountains, valleys, continents. This persists even when
the language is least dramatic:

> The mountain mists, condensing at our voice
> Under the moon, had spread their snowy flakes,
> From the keen ice shielding our linkèd sleep.
> Then two dreams came. One, I remember not.
> But in the other his pale wound-worn limbs
> Fell from Prometheus, and the azure night
> Grew radiant with the glory of that form
> Which lives unchanged within, and his voice fell
> Like music which makes giddy the dim brain,
> Faint with intoxication of keen joy.

In these lines one feels the world wandering through
space, the mountains and valleys of Asia, and the presence
of Prometheus like a Man in the Moon, symbolizing the
bowed fate of humanity.

Certain writers—Ovid is of course the supreme example
—might be classified as creators of metamorphoses. That
is to say, they develop from thought to thought, inventing
new existences with every change of mind, and then
allowing these spirits they summon from the void to vanish
into thin air. They have a tendency to create local geniuses

everywhere which personify the reasons which attract them to a place or a time. Goethe was this kind of metamorphosizing poet in the Second Part of 'Faust', more interested in the spirits he called up out of nothingness to express a changing idea than in the consistent development of his main characters. Shelley is certainly like this in 'Prometheus Unbound'. Voices spring out of the air, crystallize as a mood, and then disappear again. In this kind of pure invention of a spirit-voice, which expresses something invisible which we *feel* to be present in the universe, he compares with Shakespeare, if in no other respect. Only Ariel could have spoken the lines of the Fourth Spirit:

> On a poet's lips I slept
> Dreaming like a love-adept
> In the sound his breathing kept;
> Nor seeks nor finds he mortal blisses,
> But feeds on the aëreal kisses
> Of shapes that haunt thought's wildernesses.
> He will watch from dawn to gloom
> The lake-reflected sun illume
> The yellow bees in the ivy-bloom,
> Nor heed nor see, what things they be;
> But from these create he can
> Forms more real than living man,
> Nurslings of immortality!
> One of these awakened me,
> And I sped to succour thee.

This and other lyrics, spoken by disembodied characters, adorn 'Prometheus Unbound' like sculptures of the winds on a Greek temple.

Yet this poem, like many others of Shelley, is marred by bad construction, blurred imagery, and sheer bad writing. What could be more exasperating than to come on a 'Chorus of Spirits' which begins:

> We come from the mind
> Of human kind
> Which was late so dusk, and obscene, and blind,

> Now 'tis an ocean
> Of clear emotion,
> A heaven of serene and mighty motion.

And even a lyric which opens with the rapturous intensity
of the Goethe of *West-Oestlicher Divan*, embarrasses the
reader by the confused machinery of the images:

> Life of Life! thy lips enkindle
>   With their love the breath between them;
> And thy smiles before they dwindle
>   Make the cold air fire; then screen them
> In those looks, where whoso gazes
> Faints, entangled in their mazes.

Unless one is carried away by the sheer intensity of this, one
wonders how the last three lines work out. How can you
be screened by looks which are also mazes in which who-
ever gazes becomes entangled and faints? An image suggests
a mental structure in the mind of the reader—and how
could one draw such a picture?

I have dwelt so long on 'Prometheus Unbound' because
it is, after all, the most completely achieved and the most
happily successful of Shelley's didactic poems. 'Hellas',
though published by Shelley during his lifetime, is so sketchy
that it is difficult to understand how even he can have been
willing to see it in print.

'The Triumph of Life'—of which I have written earlier—is
the long poem on which Shelley was engaged at the time of
his death. Written, significantly, in *terza rima* it shows the
influence of Dante, and was meant, doubtless, to be Shelley's
vision of humanity, modified by a deepening knowledge of
human beings. The picture he has of life is no longer
divided so sharply into black and white, the devils and the
angels, the tyrants and the oppressed, as formerly. It is an
intermingled scene, and one may guess that the problem he
had set himself in this poem was to apply revolutionary
principles, in which he refused to lose faith, to lives in which
he had lost it:

As in that trance of wondrous thought I lay,
This was the tenour of my waking dream:—
Methought I sate beside a public way

Thick strewn with summer dust, and a great stream
Of people there was hurrying to and fro,
Numerous as gnats upon the evening gleam,

All hastening onward, yet none seemed to know
Whither he went, or whence he came, or why
He made one of the multitude, and so

Was borne amid the crowd, as through the sky
One of the million leaves of summer's bier;
Old age and youth, manhood and infancy,

Mixed in one mighty torrent did appear,
Some flying from the thing they feared, and some
Seeking the object of another's fear; . . . .

These lines show how much Shelley has mastered in English the use to which Dante put this measure in Italian. Dante's images have a transparent quality as though they were painted on glass through which light shines. Combined with the strong images it is perhaps the alternating rhymes and the lines arranged in triplets which give this effect of one thing shining through another. At times when he wants to point a conclusion, Dante uses this metre with a force which has the weight of tragic statement; and yet the light continues to glow through even the human tragedy, which is only a part of the whole pattern of the poem. Shelley achieves just this effect of making a tragic statement about humanity, which is immediately transcended, in the lines:

Some flying from the thing they feared, and some
Seeking the object of another's fear; . . . .

Shelley was a careless, but none the less a brilliant technician. The hurriedness, the frequent lapses into bad writing, the occasional defects of ear and of verbal sensibility, the blurring of images, and many other faults, should not blind one to his technical ease, which seems so great that

it perhaps deceived him into thinking that it was not
necessary for him to take pains.

(2) *Spiritual autobiographies.* Shelley's proselytizing was
obviously connected with his own problems, which had led
him from childhood to rebel against existing social con-
ventions. These problems were certainly not resolved by
his rather frustrated public activities, nor even by his relationships with men and women. One aspect of his poetry
is an endeavour to understand himself in poems which are
completely, or almost completely, isolated from his public
thought. In these poems he meditates with himself in
conscious isolation and seems to be seeking the companionship of a woman or a man with whom he can completely
identify himself. There is a strain of self-pity in most of
this writing, and a strong sense of his own sensitivity and
high moral qualities.

In 'Prince Athanase', a curious fragment written in 1817,
the opening lines already assert what is his theme in all these
writings:

> There was a youth, who, as with toil and travel,
> Had grown quite weak and gray before his time;
> Nor any could the restless griefs unravel
>
> Which burned within him, withering up his prime
> And goading him, like fiends, from land to land.
> Not his the load of any secret crime,
>
> For nought of ill his heart could understand, ...

We soon learn that this youth was gentle, aspiring, just,
innocent, loving, wedded to Wisdom, unabusive of his
position in society, an honest steward, fearless, 'scorning all
disguise', liberal, frank, indifferent to the enmity of those
who envied him, serene, etc. This is only a small part of the
catalogue of his virtues. It seems most probable that Shelley
did dramatize himself to himself as an almost perfect
character who was hated by the world only because he had
divorced his perfection from any basis of religious super-

stition. In Part II of the same poem there is a curious description of the one beloved friend of Prince Athanase, who was 'An old, old man, with hair of silver white' who —in brief—understood Athanase perfectly and tried to comfort him. This friend, Zonoras, is doubtless the father whom Shelley had failed to find in Sir Timothy, Bart.

Shelley's Preface to 'Alastor', or 'The Spirit of Solitude' reveals the same psychological situation. '. . . A youth of uncorrupted feelings and adventurous genius led forth by an imagination inflamed and purified through familiarity with all that is excellent and majestic, to the contemplation of the universe. . . . But the period arrives when these objects cease to suffice. . . . He images to himself the Being whom he loves. . . He seeks in vain for a prototype of his conception. Blasted by his disappointment, he descends to an untimely grave.'

The poet seeks, as we see, another person who is really his idealized vision of himself. Here I am not concerned with the results of this search in Shelley's life but with its effect on his poetry. For if in life he seeks his double, is he not also trying in these autobiographical poems to create his double in his poetry? Does he not bend over the strange, watery, reflecting imagery of 'Alastor', and see himself imaged within it, so that the poem is really the stream in which Narcissus loves himself? And what he meets is death within the waters where he can seek nothing but himself. The poetry leads inevitably towards a condition of merging, fainting, swooning, where the poet dies as it were within his own words, and the reader is unable to hold on to anything in the flow of evanescent imagery:

'Vision and Love!'
The Poet cried aloud, 'I have beheld
The path of thy departure. Sleep and death
Shall not divide us long!'

A curious feature of 'Alastor' is its exact prophecy of the manner of the poet's death, by drowning in his sailing boat.

'Epipsychidion' is the culmination of Shelley's autobiographical confessions, in which he is always trying to make a
pattern out of an experience which instead of bringing him
closer to others, as he feels it should do, isolates him. His
theme is once more love based on entering so completely
into the existence of another that it becomes like *being*
another. It is a love beyond question by human institutions, and which inevitably sets aside the claims of all other
people. For if you *are* another and she is you, the relationship of each with the other is simply a form of being himself or herself. The question of a physical relationship also
becomes trivial, because all forms of knowing one another
are only self-awareness.

Shelley's search for Emilia is justified in the poem by his
never having found the Being who is unquestionably his
ideal. He is in search, as it were, of a Holy Grail, and the
fact that he has believed himself to find it previously in
'many mortal forms' only justifies him in setting his past
(Harriet in her grave and Mary at home at Pisa) aside, while
he grasps it. In a beautiful and revealing passage he describes
the Being who has haunted his life, whom he believes
himself to have found in Emilia:

> There was a Being whom my spirit oft
> Met on its visioned wanderings, far aloft,
> In the clear golden prime of my youth's dawn,
> Upon the fairy isles of sunny lawn,
> Amid the enchanted mountains, and the caves
> Of divine sleep, and on the air-like waves
> Of wonder-level dream, whose tremulous floor
> Paved her light steps;—on an imagined shore,
> Under the gray beak of some promontory
> She met me, robed in such exceeding glory,
> That I beheld her not. In solitudes
> Her voice came to me through the whispering woods,
> And from the fountains, and the odours deep
> Of flowers, which, like lips murmuring in their sleep
> Of the sweet kisses which had lulled them there,
> Breathed but of *her* to the enamoured air;

And from the breezes whether low or loud,
And from the rain of every passing cloud,
And from the singing of the summer-birds,
And from all sounds, all silence.

Shelley describes his pursuit of this ideal in words which later influenced Francis Thompson describing his own pursuit by the Hound of Heaven:

Then, from the caverns of my dreamy youth
I sprang, as one sandalled with plumes of fire,
And towards the lodestar of my one desire
I flitted, like a dizzy moth, whose flight
Is as a dead leaf's in the owlet light . . .

There follows an interesting list of those whom Shelley embraced but who failed to achieve his ideal. Mary is here identified with the 'cold chaste Moon' who has left him in a 'cold chaste bed'.

The poem now turns more resolutely to Emily. There is a climax in a passage which wonderfully foreshadows Baudelaire's 'L'Invitation':

Emily,
A ship is floating in the harbour now,
A wind is hovering o'er the mountain's brow;
There is a path on the sea's azure floor,
No keel has ever ploughed that path before;
The halcyons brood around the foamless isles;
The treacherous Ocean has forsworn its wiles;
The merry mariners are bold and free:
Say, my heart's sister, wilt thou sail with me?

But the poem ends on a note where this journey has penetrated to death and despair:

One Heaven, one Hell, one immortality,
And one annihilation. Woe is me!
The wingèd words on which my soul would pierce
Into the height of love's rare Universe,
Are chains of lead around its flight of fire—
I pant, I sink, I tremble, I expire!

It is as though all the time the poet has been in pursuit of his own soul, and when he has succeeded in separating this from all earthly things—from his own body even—he achieves inanition.

Yet 'Epipsychidion' has a wonderful joyousness despite the desperate nature of this search for the Ideal. Here Shelley has pursued and exposed his own life's aims with all the logic of his poetry. The poem contains his philosophy of love, expressed in words which have profoundly influenced many people in their lives. Emily becomes the symbol for a lifetime search, and the definition of his aim is so convincing that the reader forgets it is not a definition of any possible woman. Perhaps Shelley himself no longer cared, and revelled in the opportunity to map out his own inhumanity. In this poem he came as near as is possible to expressing the inexpressible, and tracing the path where poetry tapers off into a vision which is beyond words. The poem too is a product of Italy. In it Shelley secretly joins the company of the early Renaissance poets of Romantic love.

(3) *Pure lyrics.* Shelley is best known to a public who read poets in anthologies by lyrics like 'Lines written among the Euganean Hills', 'Ode to the West Wind', 'Love's Philosophy', 'The Cloud', 'To a Skylark', 'Arethusa', 'Hymn of Pan', 'The Question', 'Music, when soft voices die'. These poems have a concreteness lacking in much of Shelley's work. Some of them develop round a single theme which reminds one of certain sonatas of Beethoven—the 'Moonlight', or 'Les Adieux'. Like Beethoven Shelley is an artist who seems to care more for the general outline and development of his theme than for the instrument he is using. He masters words rather than tames them, and shows little sense of their limitations. He invents juxtapositions of images which are almost unthinkable, just as Beethoven sometimes produces combinations of notes which suggest an intellectual idea without ever being satisfactory within the limits of what one can pleasantly hear. It is impossible to compare Shelley with poets like Pope and Dryden, without

noticing his indifference to the limitations of language. He bangs away at words in order to produce a tune and a vision above a multitude of superfluous images, or he produces— as in the concluding passages of 'Epipsychidion'—such a rapid succession of different impressions, that the reader feels that metre and words are being used as rails among which he is hurled at headlong speed without being given time to study the detail. Or if he does look too closely at single images, or examine the machinery of a metaphor, he is unsatisfied. Yet Shelley does achieve a freedom which is felt to be real. He can say things which have not been said before, and since—as I have pointed out—he sometimes verges on expressing the inexpressible, an impressionist use of language and imagery is perhaps his only resort. A stricter use of language would make a great deal of his subject-matter impossible.

The 'Ode to the West Wind', the most symphonic poem in the English language, is divided into stanzas composed in *terza rima* and cut into sonnet length. It's first movement is a magnificent invocation, the development of whose theme carries the power through the poem's first two stanzas. With the third stanza ,'Thou who didst waken from his summer dreams', there is the effect of a slow movement. The next stanza—the fourth—resumes the mood of the first, and the poem culminates in a magnificent trumpet blast—'the trumpet of a prophecy', indeed.

'Lines written among the Euganean Hills' is Shelley's most purely visual poem. From the first line 'Many a green isle needs must be' the writing is sombrely coloured, as the mariner travels on through the sea scattered with flowing islands which lie 'In the waters of wide Agony'. To my mind, this poem is Shelley's lyric masterpiece, and is not open to the usual criticisms for defects of metaphor. The metre is completely mastered, and it points towards the later Yeats in lines like:

> One white skull and seven dry bones,
> On the margin of the stones,

Where a few gray rushes stand,
Boundaries of the sea and land:
Nor is heard one voice of wail
But the sea-mews, as they sail
O'er the billows of the gale; . . . .

(4) *Confessional lyrics*. In addition to his long autobio-
graphic poems, Shelley's works are scattered with what I call
his Confessional lyrics—short occasional poems written out
of his immediate experiences. These show him in a far more
human and sympathetic light than his more sustained efforts
to justify himself. For they seem to spring out of an irrepressible urge to express some truth of an immediate feeling,
without his usual attempt to put himself in the right (one of
Shelley's biographers records only one case in his whole life
in which Shelley admitted himself to have been in the wrong
about something. He admitted in a letter that he had behaved
rather badly to Elizabeth Hitchener, the Brown Demon).

The early personal poems of Shelley have a certain simplicity which is very soothing after the turmoil of his
ambitious works. We can trace in them the story of his
love for Harriet when he wrote of her:

Thy look of love has power to calm
The stormiest passion of my soul

to the poignant 'Lines' ending with the stanza:

The moon made thy lips pale, beloved—
The wind made thy bosom chill—
The night did shed on thy dear head
Its frozen dew, and thou didst lie
Where the bitter breath of the naked sky
Might visit thee at will.

Reading these lines one understands why Shelley was
Thomas Hardy's favourite poet.

His loves appear in these poems and in the fragments 'To

Constantia Singing' and the 'Fragment to One Singing',
which foreshadows again a poem by Baudelaire:

> My spirit like a charmèd bark doth swim
> Upon the liquid waves of thy sweet singing,
> Far far away into the regions dim
>
> Of rapture—as a boat, with swift sails winging
> Its way adown some many-winding river,
> Speeds through dark forests o'er the waters swinging . . .

Then there is the beautiful poem 'To William Shelley', his
son who was to die so soon, which has a Blakeian simplicity
and innocence. The lines 'To F. G.' recall another of the
disasters which pursued Shelley:

> Her voice did quiver as we parted,
> Yet knew I not that heart was broken
> From which it came, and I departed
> Heeding not the words then spoken.
> Misery—O Misery,
> This world is all too wide for thee.

In 1819 there follow a series of poems to Mary appealing to
her to melt into kindness again from the frozen state of grief
into which she had entered as the result of the loss of her
two children. But there is a growing sense of the hopeless-
ness of looking in her direction, and of the tragedy which
neither of them could escape. As he had written already in
1818:

> Forget the dead, the past? Oh, yet
> There are ghosts that may take revenge for it,
> Memories that make the heart a tomb,
> Regrets which glide through the spirit's gloom,
> And with ghastly whispers tell
> That joy, once lost, is pain.

These personal poems by Shelley, and the fragments
scattered amongst them, are among the poems of Shelley
most sympathetic to the modern reader.

The most complete statement of his relationship with Mary, resulting in his isolation, is in 'To Edward Williams', beginning:

> The serpent is shut out from Paradise.
>> The wounded deer must seek the herb no more
>> In which its heart-cure lies:
>> The widowed dove must cease to haunt a bower
> Like that from which its mate with feigned sighs
>> Fled in the April hour.
> I too must seldom seek again
> Near happy friends a mitigated pain.

Here Shelley's self-pity has become so resigned that it acquires nobility. The language has freshness and directness, because Shelley is writing simply to relieve his feelings and to say something to his friends Edward and Jane which he perhaps could not express in conversation. He is not writing Poetry with a big P.

But in one or two of the personal lyrics, the intimate is fused with the highly poetic. 'To Jane: the Invitation' and 'To Jane: the Recollection' are a happy combination of the relaxed and conversational with a high poetic purpose. In the second of these poems, the description of the forest pools has a closeness and delicacy of word-painting which also expresses Shelley's state of mind with a rare delicacy of pathos:

> Like one beloved the scene had lent
>> To the dark water's breast,
> Its every leaf and lineament
>> With more than truth expressed;
> Until an envious wind crept by,
>> Like an unwelcome thought,
> Which from the mind's too faithful eye
>> Blots one dear image out.
> Though thou art ever fair and kind,
>> The forests ever green,
> Less oft is peace in Shelley's mind,
>> Than calm in waters, seen.

(5) *Satiric poems.* Although Shelley is not thought of as a satirist, he wrote one effective satire, 'Swellfoot the Tyrant', on the landing of Queen Caroline in England and the efforts of King George IV to refute her claims. This is well worth reading, and shows a boisterous side of Shelley which does not fit with the usual idea of his genius.

'Peter Bell the Third' is a parody on Wordsworth's much-parodied 'Peter Bell'. In Part the Third it changes from mocking imitation of Wordsworth to savage satire on London, under the significant title of 'Hell':

> Hell is a city much like London—
> A populous and a smoky city;
> There are all sorts of people undone,
> And there is little or no fun done;
> Small justice shown, and still less pity.

Writing with the mock-loonish simplicity he has borrowed from Wordsworth, Shelley shows how effective this style can be when it is savage. The manner is far more successful than his high-flown essays in moral indignation.

This Third Part of 'Peter Bell the Third' is very close in spirit to another satiric poem, 'The Mask of Anarchy', which is concerned with the Peterloo massacres near Manchester, in the autumn of 1819. Here again the form is that of the popular ballad, and the manner that of naked indignation.

VI

Two or three poems do not fall easily into the categories I have indicated. One is the famous 'Adonais', an elegy on the death of Keats. This is a monumental, stylized poem describing the spirits who mourn at the bier of the poet. It ends with the famous platonic image of 'life like a dome of many-coloured glass', which 'stains the white radiance of Eternity'. This poem is impressive as a frieze in its development and execution, but, beautiful as it is, I find the material

too heavily stylized to be entirely suited to the rapid shifts of
Shelley's sensibility. The effect is sculpture in stone, when
Shelley works best in light and air.

Light and air seem indeed the materials of the beautiful
and fantastic 'The Witch of Atlas', a poem in which Shelley
indulged his taste for pure invention. This wonderful
flight into shapes and shadows of pure moonlight annoyed
Mary; or so Shelley states in his half-malicious Preface.

Another wholly delightful, though less fanciful, excursion
is the 'Letter to Maria Gisborne', in which Shelley entertains
his friend with a picture of the people and things she will
see when she travels to London. Here he shows that even
if he could not create people, he could do perceptive and
imaginative characterizations of his contemporaries. As this
famous vignette of Coleridge:

> You will see Coleridge—he who sits obscure
> In the exceeding lustre and the pure
> Intense irradiation of a mind,
> Which, with its own internal lightning blind,
> Flags wearily through darkness and despair—
> A cloud-encircled meteor of the air,
> A hooded eagle among blinking owls.

VII

Shelley was established in the literary mind of the Nineteenth Century as a great poet. Indeed when I was at
school, I gained the impression that Great Poetry in England
began with Chaucer, continued with Shakespeare, and then
developed by means of Milton and Wordsworth directly to
Keats, Byron, and Shelley. These were the Great Poets,
and nearly everyone else was Minor.

In recent years there has been not so much a re-estimate,
as a restoring of some sense of balance in the values of
English poetry. What Byron saw already—that Pope was

a greater poet than Byron himself or any of his contemporaries—is now generally recognized. The Romantics are now under a cloud, from which they may finally emerge in a peculiar and isolated position, like the Metaphysical Poets.

To-day many critics would hesitate to give Shelley even a place beside Herbert and Vaughan. The unfinished state of most of his poems, his bad technical lapses, the lack of concreteness of much of his thought, the adolescence of his earlier ideas and their immaturity even in his last work, are all held against him.

In this essay I have tried to organize the very untidy material of his *Collected Poems*, and to present the facts of his life in such a way that the reader may have an opportunity of judging for himself. When all the untidiness and overgrowth have been cleared away, it is seen that there are a number of finished poems, and that some of these are a new development in English poetry.

The real difficulty in judging a poet like Shelley is that he does not obey in his own writing even those rules which it is possible to deduce from that writing. He does not provide the reader with his own standards, even, whereby to judge him. He uses poetry as a medium for expressing his ideas and his personal conflicts, more than he exercises it as a craft or plays it as an intellectual game.

The existence of this difficulty is in itself a serious criticism of him as an artist. But having admitted that this criticism often applies, there are also occasions on which it does not do so, and there are other occasions (in 'Epipsychidion', for example) when his wilful perversity seems justified, because the poem does, as a whole, re-create a significant experience.

One means of judging whether an artist is minor or major is to inquire into the range of the experience which he attempts to create in his work. From certain points of view, Shelley was shut out from a great deal of human experience. Matthew Arnold called him an 'ineffectual angel', and the character in Aldous Huxley's novel *Point*

Counterpoint who is supposed to represent D. H. Lawrence (and it is difficult to think that Aldous Huxley ever *invented* a character in a novel) calls him a slug. He lacked earthiness, sensuality, realism, concreteness, and his behaviour was scarcely ever natural. He was, in common with D. H. Lawrence himself, and with Proust, a highly over-spiritualized creature. But for an artist, his own nature is the channel which connects him with the world, and to judge his work we must consider not the channel but the quantity of life which—with however many twists—does go through it. A great deal of Shelley's work does simply reflect the defects of his own nature. But in a good deal he gets beyond his nature, and shows a sensitive and profound awareness of life. Besides considering separate examples, one has to make a sum of what his work as a whole adds up to. For this reason I have divided it into rough categories, in order to indicate the many-sidedness of the productivity of this poet.

Shelley is perhaps not a Great Poet, but his life-work is a sketch for a Great Poetry, and any poet who has lived after him might do ill to ignore his effort and example. In the nineteenth, and even the twentieth century, later poets are more indebted to Shelley than to any other Romantic writer. Browning's, Swinburne's, and Patmore's debts are obvious. But perhaps the most striking example of the fertilizing influence of Shelley is in Thomas Hardy's 'The Dynasts', where Hardy combined Shelley's interest in the effects of the French Revolution with his cosmic point of view, and produced the major attempt at an epic in this century. Another poet who discovered aspects of Shelley which influenced different phases of his own life-work, was Yeats. And T. S. Eliot in *The Cocktail Party* makes one of his characters quote from 'Prometheus Unbound' in order to elucidate the most difficult situation in that play.

Shelley's style is, from one point of view, of little use to a contemporary poet. That is to say, not only the subject-matter, but also the language is removed from common experience and common speech, in all but a few poems. This fault, above all, has alienated modern poets from his writing. On the other hand, he forged a language which was highly capable of expressing eloquently and beautifully abstract thought and intellectual ideas. In different circumstances, Shelley might have been held to have invented in England something corresponding to the '*dolce stil nuovo*' of the group of Italian poets immediately preceding Dante. It is possible that a more constructively critical study of his work than has yet been given us, might still illuminate for modern poets a path out of their intellectual obscurity, and show how the most complex ideas can be expressed with lucid ease.

SHELLEY

A Select Bibliography

(Place of publication London, unless stated otherwise)

Bibliography:

THE SHELLEY LIBRARY: An Essay in Bibliography, by H. Buxton Forman (1886)
—'Shelley's books, pamphlets, and broadsides; posthumous separate issues; and posthumous books wholly or mainly by him.' Issued by the Shelley Society. One of the earliest essays in modern descriptive bibliography, and still useful.

AN ALPHABETICAL TABLE OF CONTENTS TO SHELLEY'S POETICAL WORKS, by F. S. Ellis (1888)
—issued by the Shelley Society.

A LEXICAL CONCORDANCE TO THE POETICAL WORKS OF P. B. SHELLEY. Compiled and arranged by F. S. Ellis (1892).

THE SHELLEY COLLECTION. Bodleian Library, Oxford (1893)
—a catalogue of the manuscripts, printed books, and portraits comprised in the collection. Considerable accessions have been made since this catalogue was published, Sir John Shelley-Rolls having deposited in the Bodleian, in 1946, all the MSS. and papers remaining in the Shelley family.

A DESCRIPTIVE CATALOGUE OF THE FIRST EDITION IN BOOK FORM OF THE WRITINGS OF P. B. SHELLEY, 1792–1822, by R. Granniss. New York (1923)
—issued to members of the Grolier Club.

A SHELLEY LIBRARY. A catalogue of Printed Books, Manuscripts and Autograph Letters by Percy Bysshe Shelley, Harriet Shelley, and Mary Wollstonecraft Shelley, by T. J. Wise. Privately printed (1924)
—the Shelley portion of the Ashley Library, now in the British Museum.

THE SHELLEY CORRESPONDENCE IN THE BODLEIAN LIBRARY, ed. R. H. Hill. Oxford (1926)
—contains a list of Shelley manuscripts and relics in the Library.

A BIBLIOGRAPHY OF SHELLEY'S LETTERS PUBLISHED AND UNPUBLISHED, by S. de Ricci. Privately printed. Paris (1927).

AN ACCOUNT OF AN EXHIBITION OF BOOKS AND MANUSCRIPTS OF PERCY BYSSHE SHELLEY at the University of Texas. Austin, Texas (1935).

Note: In addition to the important collections in the British Museum (Ashley Library), Bodleian, and Harvard College libraries, there is a valuable collection of printed books and manuscripts by and relating to Shelley (as yet uncatalogued) in the Pforzheimer Library, Purchase, New Jersey, U.S.A.

Collected Works:

POETICAL PIECES (1823)
—a composite volume, with general title-page, containing remainders of *Prometheus Unbound*, etc., *Hellas*, and other separately published works.

THE POETICAL WORKS OF COLERIDGE, SHELLEY, AND KEATS. Paris (1829)
—the Galignani edition, with a Memoir of Shelley, by C. Redding.

THE SHELLEY PAPERS. A Memoir of Shelley by T. Medwin, and Original Poems and Papers by Shelley now first collected (1833).

THE POETICAL WORKS, ed. Mrs. Shelley. 4 vols. (1839)
—American edition with memoir by J. R. Lowell. 3 vols. Boston, Mass., 1855. Mrs. Shelley's annotations have been extensively used by all later editors.

ESSAYS, LETTERS FROM ABROAD, TRANSLATIONS AND FRAGMENTS, ed. Mrs. Shelley. 2 vols. (1840).

THE WORKS, ed. Mrs. Shelley. 2 vols. (1847).

RELICS OF SHELLEY, ed. R. Garnett (1862)
—prose, verse, and letters.

THE POETICAL WORKS, including various Additional Pieces, from MSS. and Other Sources. The Text carefully revised, with Notes and a Memoir by W. M. Rossetti. 2 vols. (1870); 3 vols. revised (1878).

THE POETICAL [AND PROSE] WORKS. Now first given from the Author's Original Editions. With hitherto Inedited Pieces and a Memoir by Leigh Hunt. Edited, with notes, by R. H. Shepherd. 4 vols. (1871-5)
—in vols. 3-4 the title is altered to 'The Works'.

POETICAL WORKS. Edited, with an Introductory Memoir, by W. B. Scott (1874).

THE POETICAL WORKS, ed. H. Buxton Forman. 4 vols. (1876–7)
—the earliest of Buxton Forman's authoritative editions of the poems. New editions in 2 vols., 1882, and in 5 vols., 1892.

THE WORKS IN VERSE AND PROSE. Now first brought together, with many pieces not before published. Edited, with Prefaces, Notes, and Appendices, by H. Buxton Forman. 8 vols. (1880) [1876–80].

SHELLEY AND MARY, ed. Sir Percy Florence and Lady Jane Shelley. With a Preface by Sir Percy Shelley. 4 vols. Privately printed (1882)
—the unpublished poems, letters, diaries, and other documents in the possession of the Shelley family.

ESSAYS AND LETTERS, ed. E. Rhys (1886).

THE POETICAL WORKS from the Original Editions. Edited, prefaced and annotated by R. H. Shepherd. 3 vols. (1888); 2 vols. (1912)
—R. H. Shepherd also edited a two volume edition of Prose Works, 1888 and 1912.

THE POETICAL WORKS, ed. E. Dowden (1890)
—with Mrs. Shelley's prefaces and notes.

COMPLETE POETICAL WORKS. The Text newly collated and revised and edited, with a Memoir, and Notes, by G. E. Woodberry. 4 vols. Boston, Mass. (1892)
—the 'Centenary Edition'.

THE POETICAL WORKS. Overseen by F. S. Ellis. 3 vols. [1894] (1895)
—the finely printed edition from William Morris's Kelmscott Press.

THE COMPLETE POETICAL WORKS, including materials never before printed in any edition of the poems. Edited, with textual notes, by T. Hutchinson. Oxford (1905)
—revised edition by B. P. Kurtz, 1934. The standard edition.

THE POETICAL WORKS. With an Introduction by A. H. Koszul (1907)
—Everyman's Library edition.

SHELLEY'S LITERARY AND PHILOSOPHICAL CRITICISM. Edited, with an Introduction, by J. Shawcross (1909).

SHELLEY'S PROSE IN THE BODLEIAN MANUSCRIPTS, ed. A. H. Koszul (1910).

THE POEMS. Edited, with notes, by C. D. Locock. With an Introduction by A. Clutton-Brock. 2 vols. (1911).

NOTE-BOOKS OF PERCY BYSSHE SHELLEY. From the Originals in the Library of W. K. Bixby. Deciphered and Transcribed and Edited with a full Commentary by H. Buxton Forman. 3 vols. Boston, Mass. (1911)
—printed for members of the Bibliophile Society.

THE LYRICAL [DRAMATIC, NARRATIVE] POEMS AND TRANSLATIONS. Arranged in Chronological Order, with a Preface, by C. H. Herford. 4 vols. (1918–27)
—the Florence Press edition.

THE COMPLETE WORKS. Newly edited by R. Ingpen and W. E. Peck. 10 vols. Julian Edition (1926–7)
—the best edition of the collected prose and verse and letters.

VERSE AND PROSE FROM THE MANUSCRIPTS OF PERCY BYSSHE SHELLEY, ed. Sir John Shelley-Rolls, Bart., and R. Ingpen. Privately printed (1934)
—these MSS. were subsequently deposited in the Bodleian Library.

SELECTED POETRY, PROSE, AND LETTERS, ed. A. S. B. Glover (1951)
—the Nonesuch Library edition.

SHELLEY AND HIS CIRCLE, 1773–1822. Vols. I and II, ed. K. N. Cameron (1961)
—documents, chiefly letters, from the Shelley collection in the Pforzheimer Library. Much of this material has hitherto remained unpublished.

Separate Works:

ORIGINAL POETRY, by Victor and Cazire [i.e. Percy Bysshe and his sister Elizabeth Shelley] (1810)
—suppressed before publication, this small pamphlet, of which 1,100 copies are said to have been printed, was known only by name until 1898 when a presentation copy to Harriet Grove was discovered at Dorchester. This copy (now in the Wrenn Library), the Huntington Library copy, and the Ashley-British Museum copy are the only ones recorded. Reprinted 1898.

POSTHUMOUS FRAGMENTS OF MARGARET NICHOLSON, ed. John Fitzvictor [i.e. P. B. Shelley assisted by T. J. Hogg]. Oxford (1810). *Verse*
—a youthful hoax, its authorship being attributed to the demented woman who made an attempt on the life of George III in 1786. Reprinted, 1877.

ZASTROZZI. A Romance (1810).

A POETICAL ESSAY ON THE EXISTING STATE OF THINGS, by a Gentleman of the University of Oxford (1811).

LINES ADDRESSED TO HIS ROYAL HIGHNESS, THE PRINCE OF WALES ON HIS BEING APPOINTED REGENT, by Philopatria Jun. (1811).

ST IRVINE: Or, The Rosicrucian. A Romance. By a Gentleman of the University of Oxford (1811).

THE NECESSITY OF ATHEISM. Worthing [1811].

THE DEVIL'S WALK: A Ballad. Dublin [1812]
—a broadside.

AN ADDRESS TO THE IRISH PEOPLE. Dublin (1812).

PROPOSALS FOR AN ASSOCIATION OF . . . PHILANTHROPISTS. Dublin [1812].

DECLARATION OF RIGHTS [1812]
—a broadside.

A LETTER TO LORD ELLENBOROUGH. Barnstaple [1812].

QUEEN MAB: A Philosophical Poem. Privately printed (1813).

A VINDICATION OF NATURAL DIET. Being one in a Series of Notes to
Queen Mab, a Philosophical Poem (1813).

A REFUTATION OF DEISM, in a Dialogue (1814).

ALASTOR: Or, The Spirit of Solitude; and Other Poems (1816).

LAON AND CYTHNA, or, The Revolution of the Golden City. A
Vision of the Nineteenth Century. In the Stanza of Spenser [1817]
—suppressed and reissued as: THE REVOLT OF ISLAM. A Poem in
Twelve Cantos (1818).

A PROPOSAL FOR PUTTING REFORM TO THE VOTE THROUGHOUT THE
KINGDOM. By the Hermit of Marlow (1817).

AN ADDRESS TO THE PEOPLE ON THE DEATH OF PRINCESS CHARLOTTE.
By the Hermit of Marlow (1817).

HISTORY OF A SIX WEEKS' TOUR THROUGH A PART OF FRANCE, SWITZER-
LAND, GERMANY, AND HOLLAND. With Letters Descriptive of a Sail
Round the Lake of Geneva, and of the Glaciers of Chamouni (1817)
—in collaboration with Mrs. Shelley.

ROSALIND AND HELEN, A Modern Eclogue; with Other Poems(1819).

THE CENCI: A Tragedy, in Five Acts (1819). *Verse*
—printed at Leghorn.

PROMETHEUS UNBOUND. A Lyrical Drama in Four Acts, with Other
Poems (1820).

OEDIPUS TYRANNUS: Or, Swellfoot the Tyrant. A Tragedy in Two
Acts (1820). *Verse*

EPIPSYCHIDION. Verses Addressed to the Noble and Unfortunate Lady
Emilia V. . . now imprisoned in the Convent of . . . (1821).

ADONAIS. An Elegy on the Death of John Keats, Author of Endymion,
Hyperion, etc., (1821; second edition, Cambridge 1829).

HELLAS. A Lyrical Drama (1822)
—the Prologue was first printed by Garnett in *Relics of Shelley*, 1862.

POSTHUMOUS POEMS (1824)
—poems gathered by Mrs. Shelley from Shelley's papers.

THE MASQUE OF ANARCHY. A Poem. Now first published, with a Preface by Leigh Hunt (1832).

[A DEFENCE OF POETRY] in *Essays, Letters from Abroad, etc.*, ed. Mrs. Shelley (1840).

[AN ESSAY ON CHRISTIANITY] in *Shelley Memorials*, ed. Lady Shelley (1859).

THE DAEMON OF THE WORLD. The First Part as published in 1816 with 'Alastor'. The Second Part Deciphered and now First Printed from his own Manuscript Revision and Interpolation in the newly-discovered copy of 'Queen Mab'. Edited by H. Buxton Forman. Privately printed (1876).

NOTES ON SCULPTURES IN ROME AND FLORENCE. Together with a Lucianic Fragment and a Criticism of Peacock's Poem 'Rhododaphne'. Edited by H. Buxton Forman. Privately printed (1879).

REVIEW OF HOGG'S 'MEMOIRS OF PRINCE ALEXY HAIMATOFF', by Percy Bysshe Shelley. Together with an Extract from 'Some Early Writings of Shelley', by Professor E. Dowden. Edited, with an Introductory Note, by T. J. Wise (1886)
—issued by the Shelley Society.

THE WANDERING JEW. A Poem, ed. B. Dobell (1887)
—issued by the Shelley Society.

A PHILOSOPHICAL VIEW OF REFORM. With an Introduction and Appendix by T. W. Rolleston (1920).

THE CELANDINE. Winchester (1927). *Verse*

ON THE VEGETARIAN SYSTEM OF DIET, ed. R. Ingpen. Privately printed (1929).

THE SHELLEY NOTE BOOK IN THE HARVARD LIBRARY, ed. G. E. Woodberry. Cambridge, Mass. (1930). *Verse*

PLATO'S BANQUET. A DISCOURSE ON THE GREEKS, ETC. Revised and enlarged from the Manuscripts by R. Ingpen. Privately printed (1931).

Letters:

SELECT LETTERS. Edited, with an Introduction, by R. Garnett (1882).

[LETTERS] TO PEACOCK IN *Peacock's Memoirs of Shelley*, ed. H. F. Brett-Smith (1909)
—contains also Peacock's *Memoirs of Shelley*.

THE LETTERS. Collected and Edited by R. Ingpen. 2 vols. (1909; New Edition, with Additions and Corrections, containing material never before collected, 2 vols. 1912; new edition 1914).

THE SHELLEY CORRESPONDENCE IN THE BODLEIAN LIBRARY, ed. R. H. Hill. With a List of other Shelley Manuscripts and Relics in the Library. Oxford (1926).

LETTERS. Selected, with an Introduction, by R. B. Johnson (1929).

SHELLEY'S LOST LETTERS TO HARRIET. Edited, with an Introduction, by L. Hotson (1930).

NEW SHELLEY LETTERS, ed. W. S. Scott (1948)
—correspondence between P. B. Shelley, T. J. Hogg, T. L. Peacock, and others.

THE LETTERS OF PERCY BYSSHE SHELLEY, ed. F. L. Jones. 2 vols. (1964)
—contains many letters never before published in a collected edition. Includes correspondence between Shelley, Harriet Shelley and Elizabeth Hitchener.

Note: For an account of the forged letters of Shelley, including the twenty-five printed in 1852 (but withdrawn before publication), with an Introduction by Robert Browning, see *Major Byron*, by T. G. Ehrsam, 1951.

Some Biographical and Critical Studies:

JOURNAL OF THE CONVERSATIONS OF LORD BYRON, by T. Medwin (1824).

LORD BYRON AND SOME OF HIS CONTEMPORARIES, by Leigh Hunt (1828)
—modified in Leigh Hunt's *Autobiography* (1850. Edited J. E. Morpurgo, 1949).

IMAGINATION AND FANCY, by Leigh Hunt (1844).

THE LIFE OF PERCY BYSSHE SHELLEY, by T. Medwin. 2 vols. (1847; a new edition, printed from a copy copiously amended and extended by the Author and left unpublished at his death. With an Introduction and Commentary by H. Buxton Forman, 1913).

THE LIFE OF PERCY BYSSHE SHELLEY, by T. J. Hogg. 2 vols. (1858; new edition, with Introduction by E. Dowden, 1906).

'Memoirs of Shelley', by T. L. Peacock. *Fraser's Magazine*, 1858–60.

RECOLLECTIONS OF THE LAST DAYS OF SHELLEY AND BYRON, by E. J. Trelawny (1858; new edition, with an Introduction by E. Dowden. 1906)
—see also the same author's *Records of Shelley, Byron, and the Author* (1878) and his *Letters*, Oxford (1910).

SHELLEY MEMORIALS, ed. Lady Shelley (1859).

'Shelley: By One Who Knew Him' [Thornton Hunt]. *Atlantic Monthly*, 1863.

MEMOIR OF PERCY BYSSHE SHELLEY, by W. M. Rossetti (1870; revised edition, with a new Preface, 1886).

SHELLEY'S EARLY LIFE, by D. F. MacCarthy (1872).

WILLIAM GODWIN: HIS FRIENDS AND CONTEMPORARIES, by C. K. Paul. 2 vols. (1876).

SHELLEY, by J. A. Symonds (1878: revised 1887)
—English Men of Letters series.

THE LIFE OF PERCY BYSSHE SHELLEY, by E. Dowden. 2 vols. (1886; new editions, 1896, 1920). Abridged, 1 vol. (1950)
—in many respects unsurpassed as a standard biography.

THE LIFE OF P. B. SHELLEY, by W. Sharp (1887)
—Great Writers series. With a summary bibliography by J. B. Anderson.

A SHELLEY PRIMER, by H. S. Salt (1887)
—see also the same author's *Shelley: A Monograph* (1888) and *Shelley: Poet and Pioneer* (1913).

ESSAYS IN CRITICISM: Second Series, by M. Arnold (1888).

GLI ULTIMI GIORNI DI P. B. SHELLEY, di G. Biagi. Firenze (1892)
—English translation '*The Last Days of Percy Bysshe Shelley*' (1898).

SHELLEY AT OXFORD, by T. J. Hogg. With an Introduction by R. A. Streatfield (1904).

SHELLEY'S VIEW OF POETRY: A Lecture, by A. C. Bradley (1908)
—English Association Leaflets, No. 4.

SHELLEY, by F. Thompson. Edited, with Notes by W. M. [Wilfrid Meynell] and an Introduction by the Rt. Hon. G. Wyndham (1909).

MEMOIRS OF SHELLEY, by T. L. Peacock, with Shelley's Letters to Peacock, ed. H. F. B. Brett-Smith (1909).

SHELLEY, THE MAN AND THE POET, by A. Clutton-Brock (1910 [1909]; revised edition 1923).

LA JEUNESSE DE SHELLEY, par A. H. Koszul, Paris (1910).

SHELLEY AND HIS FRIENDS IN ITALY, by H. M. M. Rossetti, afterwards Angeli (1911).

SHELLEY'S 'TRIUMPH OF LIFE', by F. M. Stawell (1914)
—English Association Essays and Studies, Vol. 5.

SHELLEY IN ENGLAND: New Facts and Letters from the Shelley-Whitton Papers, by R. Ingpen (1917).

SHELLEY IN EDINBURGH, by W. E. Peck. Edinburgh (1922).

SHELLEY, by O. Elton (1924).

SHELLEY AND KEATS AS THEY STRUCK THEIR CONTEMPORARIES: Notes partly from Manuscript Sources, ed. E. Blunden (1925).

SHELLEY: His Life and Work, by W. E. Peck. 2 vols. (1927).

SHELLEY-LEIGH HUNT. Edited, with an Introduction, by R. B. Johnson (1928).

A NEWTON AMONG POETS, by Carl H. Grabo (1930).

THE LIFE OF PERCY BYSSHE SHELLEY, as comprised in 'The Life of Shelley' by Thomas Jefferson Hogg, 'The Recollections of Shelley and Byron' by Edward John Trelawny, 'Memoirs of Shelley' by Thomas Love Peacock. With an Introduction by H. Wolfe. 2 vols. (1933).

SHELLEY, by R. Bailey (1934)
—Great Lives series.

AFTER SHELLEY: The Letters of T. J. Hogg to Jane Williams, ed. S. Norman. Oxford (1934).

IN DEFENCE OF SHELLEY and Other Essays, by H. Read (1936).

THE UNEXTINGUISHED HEARTH, ed. N. I. White (1938).

MARY SHELLEY, by R. Glynn Grylls (1938).

SHELLEY, by N. I. White. 2 vols. New York (1940; London 1947)
—see also Portrait of Shelley, 1945.

LETTERS OF MARY W. SHELLEY. Collected and edited by F. L. Jones. 2 vols. Norman, Oklahoma (1944).

SHELLEY: A Life Story, by E. Blunden (1946).

MARY SHELLEY'S JOURNAL, ed. F. L. Jones. Norman, Oklahoma (1947).

SHELLEY AND THE THOUGHT OF HIS TIME, by J. Barrell. Yale (1948).

SHELLEY'S SOCIALISM, by E. and E. M. Aveling. Manchester (1948).

SHELLEY'S MAJOR POETRY: The Fabric of a Vision, by C. H. Baker (1948).

THE IMAGERY OF KEATS AND SHELLEY, by R. H. Fogle. N. Carolina (1949).

THE PLATONISM OF SHELLEY, by J. A. Notopoulos (1950).

MARIA GISBORNE AND EDWARD E. WILLIAMS: Their Journals and Letters, ed. F. L. Jones. Norman, Oklahoma (1951).

THE YOUNG SHELLEY, by K. N. Cameron (1951).

SHELLEY: THE LAST PHASE, by I. Roe (1953).

AN EXAMINATION OF THE SHELLEY LEGEND, ed. N. I. White. Pennsylvania (1954).

SHELLEY AT WORK, by N. Rogers (1956).

SHELLEY'S LATER POETRY, by M. Wilson (1959).

SHELLEY: HIS THOUGHT AND WORK, by D. King-Hele (1960).